Measuring the Weather

Marc Brodfuehrer

REAL LIFE readers™

Rosen Classroom™
New York

Published in 2009 by The Rosen Publishing Group, Inc.
29 East 21st Street, New York, NY 10010

Book Design: Michael J. Flynn

Photo Credits: Cover © Stephen St. John/National Geographic/Getty Images; pp. 4–5 © Yury Asotov/Shutterstock; p. 5 (lightning) © Jhaz Photography/Shutterstock; p. 5 (sunshine) © Pichugin Dmitry/Shutterstock; p. 6 (park) © Mauro Scarone/Shutterstock; p. 6 (thermometer) © Christophe Testi/Shutterstock; p. 9 (radar map) © Carolina K. Smith, M.D./Shutterstock; p. 9 (rain gauge) © Darryl Brooks/Shutterstock; p. 10 (weather vane) © Dole/Shutterstock; p. 10 (anemometer) © Jelena Popic/Shutterstock; p. 13 © Gregory Pelt/Shutterstock; p. 14 © David Burrows/Shutterstock.

ISBN: 978-1-4358-0105-9
6-pack ISBN: 978-1-4358-0106-6

Manufactured in the United States of America

Contents

What Is Weather?

The weather is what is happening in the air. Weather is how hot or cold it is. It's wind, rain, and snow, too.

Knowing the weather can help us stay healthy. We need to know what to wear outside. Knowing the weather can keep us safe. We need to know about **dangerous** storms. **Scientists** have found ways to measure the weather and make **predictions** about it. Let's look at some of the tools they use.

It's helpful to know weather predictions.

➤

°F
°C
120
100
80
60
40
20
0
20
50
40
30
20
10
0
10
20
30

Measuring Temperature

We need the sun's rays each day to stay warm. The sun's rays heat everything on and around Earth, including the air. When Earth receives a lot of the sun's power, the air **temperature** is often high. When Earth receives less of the sun's power, the air temperature is often lower. People measure temperature with tools called **thermometers**.

This thermometer uses a liquid that goes up and down as the temperature rises and falls.

←

Measuring Rain

Did you know that there's water in the air? Tiny drops of water are all around us. Water in the air rises, cools, and forms clouds. When drops of water in the clouds become heavy, they fall as rain.

A **rain gauge** is a narrow pipe that measures how much rain falls. Some gauges also measure how fast rain falls. Weather scientists use **radar** to measure rain, too. Radar uses sounds that bounce off raindrops!

On this radar picture, heavy rainfall is shown in green.

rain gauge

anemometer
wind vane

Measuring Wind

The sun's rays warm Earth and cause wind. Some parts of Earth are heated more than other parts. Warm air rises and cooler air moves in to take its place. This process causes light and strong winds. Winds can bring clouds or blow them away.

Wind direction is measured with a **wind vane**. Wind speed and direction are measured with an **anemometer**.

Wind can move weather from place to place, so it's important to know its direction and speed.

Saving Lives

Have you ever watched the weather report on TV? Weather scientists use maps, computers, and other special tools to make weather predictions. They predict dangerous storms, such as **hurricanes**, that can hurt people and buildings. They can help people prepare for travel. Weather scientists are not always right, but their weather predictions often help save lives.

During a hurricane, people need to stay in a safe place. Predicting hurricanes can save lives.

How Radar Helps

1. It's important to use tools to measure weather.
2. Weather tools can measure dangerous storms.
3. Radar can measure hurricanes.
4. Radar can track a hurricane's path.
5. Radar helps keep us safe from a hurricane.

Weather Tools

- **rain**
  - **rain gauge** measures how much rain and sometimes how fast it falls
  - **radar** measures where rain is and its strength as it falls
- **wind**
  - **wind vane** measures wind direction
  - **anemometer** measures wind speed and direction
- **temperature**
  - **thermometer** measures heat in the air

Glossary

anemometer (aa-nuh-MAH-muh-tuhr) A tool that measures wind speed and direction.

dangerous (DAYN-juh-ruhs) Unsafe.

hurricane (HUHR-uh-kayn) A storm with very strong wind and lots of rain.

prediction (prih-DIHK-shun) The act of saying what will happen before it does.

radar (RAY-dahr) A tool that uses sound waves to find an object.

rain gauge (RAYN GAYJ) A tool that measures how much rain falls in a place.

scientist (SY-uhn-tihst) A person who studies the way things are and the way things act.

temperature (TEHM-puhr-chur) How hot or cold something is.

thermometer (thur-MAH-muh-tuhr) A tool that measures how hot or cold something is.

wind vane (WIND VAYN) A tool that measures wind direction.

Index

Due to the changing nature of Internet links, The Rosen Publishing Group, Inc., has developed an online list of Web sites related to the subject of this book. This site is updated regularly. Please use this link to access the list: **http://www.rcbmlinks.com/rlr/weath**